Wholeness and the Fruits of the Spirit

Pastor John

ISBN-13: 978-1477568774

ISBN-10: 1477568778

Note – British spelling is used throughout this book as the author lives and works in Scotland.

CONTENTS

INTRODUCTION

But the fruit of the Spirit is love, joy, peace, patience, kindness, goodness, faithfulness, gentleness, self-control; against such things there is no law. (Galatians 5:22-23 English Standard Version Anglicised)

The letter to the Galatians contains a list of the nine fruits of the spirit that should be visible in the life of a Christian. These fruits are the result of the interior work of the Holy Spirit. In the natural world fruit comes from plants that are healthy, growing and fertile. The fruit of the spirit are virtues that the bible taught should be expected as signs of a Godly life. They were valued and praised by the Jews long before the birth of Christ. The fruits of the spirit could be said to be the signs of an integrated and whole person. They are the symptoms of someone who is living a fully human life.

But this begs the question of what does "fully human" mean? To be fully human is wrapped up in the Hebrew word *shalom* which means *completeness, wholeness, health, peace, welfare, soundness, tranquillity, prosperity, perfectness, fullness, rest, harmony.* In short, it is the absence of disharmony, agitation, dis-ease and disease, and fragmentation. It involves awareness of our oneness with our God, as known in the trinity, and with one another. Today there is much concern with wholeness which shows itself in such things as holistic medicine, and the search for a perfect integration of body, mind and spirit. This is due to a fundamental longing in the secular world where people feel "there must be more to life than just this". As a result an industry has grown up to provide self help books and courses to help people find happiness and fulfillment. As a Christian I believe wholeness comes through a life lived in imitation of Jesus Christ, the most whole and perfect person that ever lived.

This short book in its ten chapters will look at wholeness in terms of the fruits of the Spirit working themselves out in the lives of Christian people. I hope it will help Christians become more integrated and whole people and so find the life in all its fullness that Jesus promises. It originated as a series of sermons preached a lifetime ago in 1993 but has been revised many times since then.

Pastor John 2012

1 LOVE

"Whoever loves is a child of God and knows God." 1 John 4:7

Long ago, I remember a television programme called "Butterflies". It was a romantic comedy series. It was of special interest to me because it had been filmed on the streets of Cheltenham in Gloucestershire where I grew up. Though this kind of tragic comedy isn't really my cup of tea, I find that I still am haunted by the words of the song that was used for the signature tune.

Love is like a butterfly,
as soft and gentle as a sigh
the multi-coloured moods of love
are a rare and precious thing

Though the tune is slushy and sentimental and the words gush with romantic mush there is something profound about this verse. I believe that it can help us to understand the power of the biblical image of love. That image is most dramatically described as the central part of the Christian life in the familiar bible passage from the first letter of John. (Read the whole letter if you have time.)

Beloved, let us love one another, because love is from God; everyone who loves is born of God and knows God.... The commandment we have from him is this: those who love God must love their brothers and sisters also. (1 John 4: 7 and 21)

The fragile strength of love

That little phrase from the song "Love is like a butterfly" says something about love's strength – fragile and strong. Love it is true can be "as soft and gentle as a sigh" as the song goes but there is also immense strength there. If a butterfly were too soft it would never fly. Its wings though delicate in our sight are immensely strong and muscular membranes which enable the creature to fly. If you were a giant the wings of an airplane would look small and feeble when you think of the weight they support in the air. I marveled at the possibility of flight last week as I looked out of the plane window on the way home from a trip overseas. We know that planes are carefully and precisely engineered to deal with the stresses and pressures that they have to face going through the air. How much more wonderful then are a butterflies wings, which God has planned to give the maximum efficiency and power to the creature.

Love is soft and gentle but love is also the most powerful and strong emotion known to men and women. Just think, there would be no plots for romantic novels if heroes and heroines were not willing to take great risks for the sake of their loved ones. Strength isn't always what it seems to be. I don't suppose you would think of a spiders web as one of the strongest constructions on the earth but apparently in scale it is. It is so strong that the American military have been using chemicals from spiders web weaving glands to grow spiders web fabric in the laboratory to make new compounds and materials where strength and lightness is needed. (for example for parachutes and aircraft) Love looks soft and fragile but love is very strong.

The bible recognises that of all the virtues *"The greatest of these is love"* (1Cor 13:13). Love is what holds together all the other parts of the Christian life *"Over all these virtues put on love which binds them together in perfect unity"* (Col3:14).

The multi-coloured moods of love

A line in the song reminds us that love has many multi-coloured moods. There was a cartoon series that had a picture with the caption "love is" in the newspaper my parents used to get every day when I was a boy. I haven't seen it recently as I look at different newspapers these days. There are many times when the bible says love is... and not just in 1 Corinthians 13 which is the most popular reading on love in all scripture but there are many other references. So from the bible we find many helps to understand the breadth of the meaning of love and so understand more fully what love is.

First of all Love is not something that should be kept in the family and close friends. Love should go beyond our personal preferences. The Old testament told us that Love is impartial *"And you are to love those who are aliens, for you yourselves were aliens in Egypt"* (Duet10.19). The people of Israel from an early time knew that God wanted them, to be generous and inclusive in their love They frequently fell short of this ideal. Jesus went further and said that we are to love our enemies. This sounds alright when we say it quickly because most of us don't have real enemies. But if you think of first century Palestine, occupied as it was by the Roman army you can see what a revolutionary and surprising thing that was to say. How would the people in the various republics that were part of the Soviet Union have reacted when told to love the Soviet army that was occupying and suppressing their people. Love them! You must be joking would be the reply. How much do we love the Taliban or al-Qaeda? Yet the bible promises that love casts out fear. So if we could truly love then we could love as Christ loved and not be afraid.

Love is unselfish

"Love your neighbour as yourself" (Matt 22:39) Of course we have to love ourselves, and then love others as much as we love ourselves. Love isn't something that we keep to ourselves. It has to be shared. There are some people who find it difficult to love themselves but I have found that with loving support, counselling and prayer, self-hatred can be healed.

You can't pretend love.

St Paul reminds us that Love is sincere *"Love must be sincere. hate what is evil, cling to what is good."* (Rom12:9) You sometimes meet people who pretend affection, pretend to be happy to see you, pretend to be upset because they feel that they should be upset. (I saw a notice on the wall of a guest house – we love all our visitors – some when they come and some when they go!) And sometimes folks can fool nearly everyone. But you cannot really pretend love. For love show itself in all parts of life. You cannot pretend everything all the time. Insincere love will be seen through sooner or later.

It is Jesus Christ himself who shows us how to love *"Love each other as I have loved you"* (John 15:12) It is by modeling ourselves on Jesus as we read of him in the bible that we find out what love means in practice. I had a friend who was a trekkie. He was one of those people who meet together in conventions where they dress up as Star Trek characters and discuss their adventures. These people are modeling themselves on another character for a moment of escapism. It is a weekend of fantasy away from the real world. It is done for a bit of fun. Modeling ourselves on Jesus is about doing what we do in the ordinary everyday routines of life, but doing it differently because we do it with love. That is not fantasy or escapism. It is there in midst of the reality of life.

For Christians, love is the way that people outside the church see we are disciples *"By this will all men know that you are my disciples, that you love one another"* (John 13:35). I hope that is the case. When I was driving past a Baptist church when I was on holiday I could have said you could tell that they were Christians by their hats!! (That is a joke!) It has to be by love that we are recognised. Love shows itself in various ways: in our attitudes to each other, in our welcome of new people to the church, in our giving, and in our concern about the problems of the world. In all these things we show our love.

Its a rare and precious thing

And the third truth about love that I want to draw out of that slushy song is that Love is a precious thing. The bible reading from the first letter of John explains this well. Love is precious because it comes from and expresses more than anything else the mind and will of God. We all know the famous text *"God so loved the world that he gave..."* (John3:16) which summarises that Jesus came because of God's love for us. From the earliest times the people of Israel had been taught that they should love God because God loved them. *"Love the Lord your God with all your heart and soul and strength"* (Deut 6.5) So we love because God first loved us.

The Jesus of John's gospel reminds us *"As the Father has loved me, so have I loved you. Now remain in my love"* (John 15:9) Jesus's love didn't die when he died, but lives on as Jesus lives on and so today we too live in that love. John said in his first letter *"Whoever lives in love lives in God and God in him"* (1John4:16) and that text, better than any other, illustrates the very close relationship between God and love. There is a line in a hymn which goes "God is love, and where true love is, God himself is there." No-one can love God and hate another person. If you love God then your whole attitude will be loving. The Christian life should be a life characterised by love in all things and in all ways.

We might try and love God but unless we can love ourselves and love others we will have so many emotional barriers to cross we will not be able to get to love God.

2 JOY

What is joy?

If we start by looking at the dictionary definition of joy we find "intense gladness: the cause of this; vivid emotion of gladness or pleasure". So even in its everyday use "Joy" is more than just the everyday emotion of happiness describing being happy. It is an intense and vivid expression of gladness and pleasure. And it is also the cause of this vivid emotion.

If joy is supposed to be a characteristic of Christians why then do we so often see such long faces in church? Sometimes we can become so worn down by the harshness and unpleasantness of much of life that we forget what joy is. In a church context it is often the case that the most committed, dedicated and involved will have the longest faces. They will be oppressed by the pressure of endless committees, the worries of church heating systems, a leak in the Sunday School roof, and concerned about unexpected funny noises from inside the organ. On top of all these church concerns, committed, dedicated and involved people will still have all the normal everyday worries that everyone shares in today's world. When these factors are added to a belief that we must take worship seriously, and when this is interpreted to mean that we have to look solemn, then it is no wonder that the most dedicated people in a church can have long faces. It is the more marginally committed people who have a constant smile on their faces. Neither type of person is experiencing joy in the Christian sense. They should be though for if we look in the bible we find that joy is the promise of God.

Joy is promised

This promise can be seen through the whole of the bible. In the book of the prophet Isaiah the writer looks to the coming restoration of the kingdom and prophesies *"They will enter Zion with singing; everlasting joy shall crown their heads. Gladness and joy will overtake them, and sorrow and sighing will flee away."* (Isa35:10) Joy here is recognisable as the human emotion that comes with great pleasure and gladness at a happy event. It was natural that the people would be happy when their nation was restored.

It is in the book of Psalms that the promise of joy becomes more explicit. In Psalm 16 for example *"You have made known to me the path of life; you will fill me with joy in your presence, with eternal pleasures at your right hand."* (Ps16:11) Being in the presence of God is clearly linked to being filled with joy. It is simply the presence of God that can give us joy when we are aware of it. This of course doesn't mean that we aren't joyful because of the things that God does for us too. *"The lord has done great things for us and we are filled with joy"* (Ps126:5). Even in the times when we are not aware of God's presence we can rejoice for we can remember what God has done for us in the past. Then in Psalm 132 comes a promise to the priests and saints of Israel. *"I will clothe her priests with salvation and her saints shall ever sing for joy."* (Ps132:16). God's saints it foretells will ever want to sing for joy. In the New Testament of course we know that the word saint is used to describe Christians. St Paul especially used this old testament word that referred to the holy people of God and applied it directly to the followers of Jesus. Singing can be the clearest expression of joy. Think of when a child spontaneously bursts into song: it is like a great bubble of joy bursting out of them.

The prophet Nehemiah reminds us that the joy which God promises to us is not just an emotion. *"This day is holy to our lord; do not grieved, for the joy of the Lord is your strength."* (Ne8:10) It forms part of the backbone or the strength of God's people; it gives inner strength to life. Joy is essential for a fulfilled and wholly integrated life.

The promise of Joy for God's people continues into the New Testament. Jesus himself says, *"Until now you have not asked for anything in my name. Ask and you will receive, and your joy will be complete."* (Jn16:24) God has the power to make joy complete in us through Jesus who can fulfill our needs when we ask in his name.

St Paul uses the promise of joy to describe the kingdom of God in this world. *"For the kingdom of God is not a matter of eating and drinking, but of righteousness, peace and joy in the holy spirit."* (Rom14:17) In writing this Paul was rejecting the idea that specific codes of conduct, such as what you eat, characterise what it means to have entered the kingdom of God. Instead the evidence of the kingdom of God is seen in the outworking of the fruit of the spirit, especially in the presence of joy in a persons life.

From all these parts of the bible we seen that God promises his people joy. If we keep to the biblical definition of joy, can we think of anything else that promises such an experience. Holiday brochures promise enjoyment, some such as those targeted at young singles promise "fun", concert programmes promise aesthetic pleasure. Other activities provide thrills. Alex Comfort's popular book from the nineteen seventies "The Joy of Sex" used the word wrongly, implying that joy was equivalent with sensuous pleasure.

Joy can be found in sensuous pleasure when in the context of an appropriate relationship. Joy comes through relationships. It can come though family events such as marriage, the gift of a baby to a family, or the return of a lost son (as in the story of the prodigal son). Joy comes as a result of the fulfillment of human relationships in love. Wherever true love is found, there joy will be also.

Lost joy will be restored

Joy can be an extreme emotion that does not stay with us all the time at fever pitch but, when lost, joy will be restored by God. Christian joy isn't an escape from reality into a fantasy bliss state. We who experience joy still get hurt, upset, and angry. Christians whose eyes have been opened by the holy spirit will get upset and angry more often because they will be aware of the injustices and sufferings of those about them. The history of Israel is also full of ups and downs, defeats and victories, joy lost and joy restored.

Psalm 30 is perhaps one of the best examples of complete trust in God to restore lost joy *"You turned my wailing into dancing; you removed my sackcloth and clothed me with joy,"* (Ps30:11) and again *"For his anger lasts only a moment but his favour lasts a lifetime; weeping may remain for a night but rejoicing comes in the morning."* (Ps30:5) Here we see supreme confidence that God will restore to a weeping heart the joy that was lost.

Isaiah too looked beyond the peoples immediate suffering to show how things would be. *"...provide for all those who grieve in Zion - to bestow on them a crown of beauty instead of ashes, the oil of gladness instead of mourning and a garment of praise instead of a spirit of despair."* (Isa61:3) Jeremiah makes exactly the same promise *"I will turn their mourning into gladness and give them comfort and joy instead of sorrow."* (Jer31:13) God's word through the whole of the Old Testament period was a promise and hope of joy to be restored in times of sadness and suffering. These words offer us assurance when we loose the immediacy of the experience of joy that the loss will be a temporary one and joy will return.

Jesus himself foretold his own passion and resurrection in such terms. *"I tell you the truth, you will weep and mourn while the world rejoices. You will grieve but your grief will turn to joy."* (Jn16:20) The disciples were devastated by their loss but their joy would be restored and would be greater than before.

I love strawberries but no strawberries taste like Scottish strawberries! Yet they are only with us for a short while. Each year I look forward to their short season. And each year I say farewell to that season with sadness, knowing that it will return. (I am delighted that the extensive use of poly-tunnels means that the season is now much longer than it was in my grandparents day!) Joy is not the permanent state for us. If it were it would become over-familiar and thereby tawdry. It is lost by trouble, stress, and tragedy. God's promise is that it will return if we remain close to him.

We share joy of Christ

The most important thing for a Christian is that we share joy of Christ himself. Jesus was full of joy because of his closeness with God. Luke records, *"At that time Jesus, full of joy through the holy spirit, said, 'I praise you father lord of heaven and earth because you have hidden these things from the wise and the learned and revealed them to little children.'"* (Lk10:21) Jesus' joy was a gift from the Holy Spirit because of his closeness to the Father. In John's gospel Jesus makes it clear that this joy is not something he wants to keep to himself, rather he wants his disciples to share it with him. *"I have told you this so that my joy may be in you and that your joy may be complete."* (Jn15:11) Even when Jesus was preparing for the end, in the long prayer in Johns gospel called the farewell discourse, he explains that *"I say these things while I am still in the world, so that they may have the full measure of my joy within them."* (Jn17:13)

In the teaching of the letters of the New Testament there too is an explanation of the passion of Christ in terms of joy. *"Let us fix our eyes Jesus, the author and perfecter of our faith, who for the joy set before him endured the cross, scorning its shame, and sat down at the right hand of the throne of God."* (Heb12:2) Jesus gave up the prospect of earthly joy for greater heavenly joy and communion with the father. The joy that he experienced on earth and told us that we could share is only a foretaste of the joy to come.

I believe that the most important reference to joy in the new testament comes in 1Peter. "*Though you have not seen him you love him; and even though you do not see him now, you believe in him and are filled with an inexpressible and glorious joy.*"(1Pet1:8) The natural result of our love and belief in Jesus is glorious joy. I said earlier that it is in the context of earthly human loving relationships that joy is found. Where love is, there will be joy. If this is so for human relationships, how much more true it will be for our relationships with God. For in Jesus God loves us more than any other person does.

Julian of Norwich wrote many centuries ago *"He will never have full joy in us until we have full joy in him, truly seeing his lovely blessed face."* Joy for a Christian is a gift from God. It comes when we are united with Christ, when our intellect feelings, emotions, and spirituality are combined in harmony in the power of the holy spirit. Joy comes from wholeness and wholeness comes from our relationship with God.

3 PEACE

"A heart at peace gives life to the body" Prov 14.30

Everyone wants peace. There are many situations we hear about on the news where there is no peace. Peace comes from outward security, that is knowing that you are safe from attack. People need such security to live in safety with their families and to enjoy normal life. There is another sort of peace: internal peace which is the subject of this chapter. You can live in a comfortable house, on a quiet street with all the possessions that society expects us to have acquired and still you may not be at peace. Your mind may be in a turmoil; full of unresolved conflicts, fears, and worries. Inner peace is a great blessing but it is not something that is only given to the great saints of who have perfected the art of prayer. The promise of Jesus is that peace is for everyone. Peace does not provide an easy escape from worries nor does it promise an easy conscience but it brings strength from a deep inner tranquility. It is a gift of the spirit.

Experiencing the peace of God is like nothing else. Real quiet is frightening. Have you ever been anywhere where it is totally quiet? In the country at night you may still hear the wind, the cry of some small creature, or a stream. The silence will not be absolute. The only time I've experienced it was in an underground vault. My ears didn't feel right for there was nothing. There was not even a hiss from the air conditioning to be heard. It was weird and quite scary. However quiet we may get in life, even if we can experience absolute silence, it is not the same as the peace of God.

When we say we want peace it may mean a longing to get away from other people. To escape from the noise and bustle of everyday life and from work and its pressures. We go on vacation to resorts where according to our taste, inclinations and budget we can get away from it all and experience whatever sort of peace or other noise we want. But this is not the same as the peace of God either.

Going on a silent retreat is a way of becoming quiet but it is not the stillness or lack of speech, that helps us to experience the peace of God. This comes from acknowledging the presence of God himself.

Peace is not like a blithe innocence of possible surrounding danger. Once in Ireland I went for a drive and we had a very pleasant afternoon passing through some lovely countryside. I was unsure of where we were most of the time. I enjoyed every minute of the little country lanes and small villages. When we got back, one of my passengers was white. She hadn't said anything for most of the trip. She had known where we were though. We had been driving through South

Armagh, known by the army as "bandit country". This happened in the nineteen eighties, at the time of the troubles. It was an area where policemen only traveled in armoured cars with helicopter support. They say ignorance is bliss but this is not like the peace of God. The peace of God may be with us in difficult situations to calm our minds but it never dulls us to the reality of the events around us. If anything it heightens our awareness.

The Old Testament prophets were very aware that there were false claims as to what constituted peace. Listen to Jeremiah - *"they have healed the wound of my people saying peace peace when there is no peace"*(Jer 6 :14) or Ezekial *"Because they have misled my people saying there is peace when there is no peace"*(Eze 13:10). Amos goes further and says *"Woe to those who are at ease in Zion and to those who fell secure on the mountain of Samaria"* (Amos 6:1) meaning that peace is much more than just taking your ease.

Peace is a desire of all. All through Old Testament it is desired in many places. *"In peace I will both lie down and sleep; for thou alone, O Lord, makest me dwell in safety"*(Ps4:8) Peace was both and inner and an external experience in Old Testament times for the people of Israel didn't draw a distinction between sacred and secular parts of life or society. Their outer security and their inner peace were closely related. Peace was seen as a gift from God *"may the Lord bless his people with peace"*(Ps29:11).

It is our duty to seek peace. *"Seek peace and pursue it"* says the psalmist (Ps 34:14) For Christians the instruction is more specific. *"Let the peace of Christ rule in your hearts."* says St Paul in Colossians (Col3:15) but in practical terms what does this mean.

We all know that peace comes from Christ: *"Peace I leave with you, my peace I give to you; not as the world gives do I give to you. Let not your hearts be troubled, neither let them be afraid."* (John 14:27) Familiar words which are often used as a source of comfort in funeral services. Or again from Johns gospel *"I have said this to you, that in me you may have peace"*(John16:33) Inner peace comes clearly through our relationship with God through Jesus. St Paul put it well *"Therefore since we are justified by faith, we have peace with God through our Lord Jesus Christ"* (Rom 5:1) Peace with God is the source of true inner peace. If we can be at peace with God then we can also be at peace with ourselves and with other people. As it is put in Ephesians *"For he is our peace, who has made us both one, and has broken down the dividing wall of hostility"* (Eph2:14) Peace comes through resting secure in your relationship with God. Being confident that underneath is the support of the everlasting arms. Following on from this comes the confidence to be secure in all your other relationships.

'Peace passes human understanding" is said in Philipians (Php 4:7) and in some of the wordings of our benedictions from this source. This is indeed true. It is a feeling yet more than a feeling like a stomach ache. It is a sense of calm well-being that isn't about your medical condition, nor about your physical fitness, mental state, tiredness or alertness. It is the peace of God, something like nothing else and not comparable to anything else.

Such peace was known in Old Testament times. The psalmist wrote *"great peace have those who love thy law"* (Ps 119:165) Israel's devout people found great peace from following the law which was the way of their faith. In Jesus we have an easier way. We need to set our hearts and minds on spiritual things through Jesus Christ and learn like st Paul that *"to set the mind on the spirit is life and peace"* (Rom 8:6) This is the Kingdom of God here and now with us. St Paul, again from Romans says *"For the kingdom of God is not food and drink but righteousness and peace and joy in the Holy Spirit."* (Rom 14:17) Gods Kingdom manifest here in our midst is characterised by righteousness, right conduct and behaviour. Peace is the inner calm from knowing God linked to Joy which is the great happiness at knowing that you are right with God.

In the book of proverbs is written *"a heart at peace gives life to the body"* (Prov 14:30) We too can find that inner peace is the source of the fulness of life that Jesus promised to all who believe in Him. All it takes is deepening our relationship of trust with God and seeking his presence with us at all times.

Deep inner peace is a resource given by God that strengthens us at the times of most need. At other times we may not be aware of it. I was aware of the peace of God when one of my fellow students in theological seminary tried to kill me. We were on the motorway in the fast lane doing about 75mph when his car tyre had a blow out. The car skewed into the central reservation, hit the barrier, span round in a circle and then came to rest in the centre lane, facing the way we had come. I was in the front passenger seat. I was calm as I saw the world spinning round in front of me. I remember the words of the prayer that came to my lips. I remember saying "I think we had better get out". We all got out and walked over to the side of the highway. All the traffic had stopped and there was an eerie quiet. A kind lady appeared from nowhere with a flask and gave us all some tea and then the police arrived. It might not have been like that.. We might not have all got out without a scratch. We did and God's peace was really with me on that day and kept me calm and I felt tremendously at peace and was thus able to help the others, especially the driver, who was suffering from shock. A heart at peace is a tremendous gift from God and it is a gift of the spirit that is free to us all.

4 PATIENCE

My Grandmother had many funny sayings, one of which was "Patience and water gruel's are good for gout." I never understood that one but another of hers was much easier to understand:

"*Patience is a virtue,*
Find it if you can,
For its seldom in a woman
And never in a man."

Is patience really such a rare virtue? As a fruit of the spirit it is commended to us as something that we should be practising in our lives. Patience certainly was on my mind as I wrote this chapter at the time that westerners were being held as long term hostages in Lebanon. That episode is now long past but if anyone is interested in an example of patience read the stories of the hostages of Beirut and their families who waited at home. The families had to carry on for years without knowing if their loved ones were alive or dead. And the hostages themselves have probably had to spend all their time in one room, possibly alone, often blindfolded, waiting, hoping and not daring to hope too much. In comparison with those families have gone through what on earth can patience mean for us. It seems so mundane to be patient when we aren't faced with such tragedy.

Patience is commanded

There are many places in the bible where patience is recommended as a virtue to be cultivated. The book of proverbs recognises that the source of patience is wisdom (Prov 19:11), that a patient man has great understanding (Prov 14:29), a patient man calms a quarrel (Prov 15:18) and that a patient man is better than a warrior (Prov 16:32). In those early times patience was greatly prized as an attribute of a wise man. It was seen both as a symptom of a godly life and as something practical and useful.

Perhaps the clearest instruction of all comes in the letter of James where it says *"Be patient then brothers until the Lord's coming. See how the farmer waits for the land to yield its valuable crop and how patient he is for the autumn and spring rains."*(James 5:7) Any sort of planting and waiting for the results to grow has to involve patience. Nature moves at its own speed and you can't hurry it on. Though you can use all sorts of techniques to trick plants to grow more quickly, for example by putting them in a hot house or keeping them in the dark, or feeding them with concentrated fertiliser, they still grow in a set way and we have to patiently wait for the results. James was concerned, as were many people at that time, that the Lord Jesus would immediately be returning to earth. By the time he wrote his letter it seemed as if the wait might be longer than some thought. So he was counseling the people to be patient as God would work in his own good time and God's work can not be accelerated by whatever we do to try to influence him. So here patience is urged as a way of controlling your enthusiasm for a good thing that is going to happen some time in the future when you have no control over the timing.

The letter the Romans goes further and commands people to be *"patient in affliction"*. In a situation where people were being persecuted of suffered difficulties for their faith then patience was commanded as the right response. Forbearance or perseverance are acceptable alternative translations. When things don't go as you hoped they would though you know that you are doing the right thing then the instruction is to hang on in there, do not give up, and wait. If you are doing that which is right then things should be alright in the end.

The letter to the Ephesians tells the Christians in the divided church to *"be patient, forbearing one another in love, eager to maintain the unity of the Spirit in the bond of peace."* (Eph 4:2-3) There was disagreement and division amongst people in Ephesus and they are advised to be patient with one another. From our own experience we can all recall situations where there has been a breakdown in relationships that patient forbearance would have averted. If we have patience with other people we can make allowances for them as they make allowances for us.

Patience is therefore valued as a human virtue and commended for us to attain. But the word patience seems very old fashioned somehow as much of life today is about having what you want now! The whole marketing system is set up to feed instant gratification. There is a buy now pay later culture for everything but with the experience of crashes and credit crunches then many people found out that living beyond your means was not a sensible thing to do.

Why be patient?

In Ecclesiastes it was recognised that *"The end of the matter is better than the beginning and patience is better than pride"* (Ecc7:8). Patience is about finishing what we start to do. Patience is clearly linked to perseverance. You have probably all met people who are always starting something but never seem to finish anything. People who are always full of promise but more often than not the promise appears illusory. Starting most things is easy. Having the strength, patience, perseverance to finish is much more difficult.

There is much in the Christian life that seems to bring no reward. Many times we do things when we would much rather be doing something else if we were completely honest, but still we carry on. This has always been the case. Did not St Paul write to the Galatians "*Let us not become weary in doing good, for at the proper time we will reap a harvest if we do not give up.*" (Gal6:9) God's rewards come on God's own timescale and not on our own.

Being a servant of Jesus Christ gives us a life's work, and the work that we begin may not seem to have a tidy end to it. It may be that it will be completed by others after we are gone. I received a tract in the post some years ago from a person whom was very impatient with the church for the lack of progress in a year of evangelism. He wrote pages arguing that six months had already gone by and people in churches were still sitting in their pews and doing nothing. That man had a burden of evangelism laid on his heart but couldn't put it into context of all the rest that the church had to do. I knew there were many plans being developed and we would be making an impact but we needed proper preparation. It seemed to me that here was a man trying to make God work on his time scale and couldn't see the broader perspective of salvation history.

We need patience to endure, to see things through to the end, and when working for the things of God, to let God work on his own timescale and not try to impose on God our own ideas of how quickly God should work .

The result of living patiently

Canon Vanstone's book "The Stature of Waiting" is a classic. His argument in that book is that we see in the life of Jesus two distinct stages. The first stage is his active ministry when Jesus was in command. Here Jesus set the agenda and led. The second stage comes after Jesus had been handed over and then Jesus no longer is in command. Jesus then has the agenda set for him by others. And Jesus is led rather than in the lead. The same is true for us. There are parts of life that we have control over, which we can influence and where we are free agents to do as we choose. There are other parts of life where others choose for us, where others lead us. When you are ill for example you put yourself in the hands of the medical experts. They look after you. They decide what is best for you. You cease to have much say in your destiny. In hospital maybe the only choice you have is what you will have as the menu sheet comes round for you to tick your selection for lunch tomorrow. There is joke in rather black humour - "you have to be patient to be a patient!"

Patience is the best way of dealing with those parts of life over which we have no control. It is about trusting God. We can see what happens to people who worry endlessly about things over which they have no control. There is a state of mind that comes with Christian wholeness where you are content with what we do not have in your immediate power to change.

There are somethings that it is right to be impatient about such as injustice, cruelty and suffering. When we see things that are wrong in the world we should be concerned about them. We should be concerned to do what we can to alleviate suffering as quickly as possible.

But how do we decide what we should wait patiently for and what we should be impatient about. If we are worried about this then perhaps we haven't understood that patience is about being at peace with God. What matters is what we are waiting for. Waiting for God will be rewarded.

If we are happy in our relationship to God and other people then we can be content in this life. We can experience peace of mind. We will know that we have the important things and we should not worry about those things that we can't have at the moment. Being patient and waiting on God is about a peaceful state of mind, waiting for God in the sure confidence that he will hear and answer.

"Be still before the Lord, and wait patiently for him; fret not yourself over him who prospers in his way, over the man who carries out evil devices" (Ps 37:7) Waiting patiently for God is disrupted by our fretting if we see others doing better than we are. Envy and jealousy creep in and disturb our peace of mind and contentment. Patience demands that we have the peace of minds to wait for God, content with life or else we find it difficult to get through to Him.

The promise is sure. *"I waited patiently for the Lord; he inclined to me and heard my cry."* (Ps 40:1) If we wait on God he will hear us. Patience is a virtue. It is something that will bring us great contentment whereas a lack of it will cause us disturbance. Its not easy to learn, it is worth it. But as a fruit of the spirit, with God working in us then it should become more evident if the spirit is working in our lives.

When I was 15 my grandma gave me an old bookcase. It was Victorian I think. I stripped the brown paint off it and painted it with a tin of cheap mahogany stain in one afternoon. I bought some big knobs for the doors and I was proud of my newly created antique. A few months ago I looked seriously at the old bookcase. It looked hideous, but there was something appealing about the shape that made me think about saving it. The cheap varnish looked still as if it had just been slapped on, which indeed it had. So over several weeks, using varnish stripper, sandpaper, french polish, and wood oils, I reworked the bookcase. With new handles it now looks like a reasonable piece of Victorian furniture. It wasn't until I recognised the difference in time it took me doing the job first time and doing it properly second time that I knew over the years I had learned some patience. If we can begin to see this in little things then it surely will be there in bigger and more important things too.

There is a prayer which I believe originates from alcoholics anonymous and it is something like:

God grant me the grace to change what I can control,
Patience to live with what I can't control
And wisdom to tell the difference.

5 KINDNESS

Introduction

Kindness is very difficult to speak about as everyone knows what it is. When someone says she's a real Christian they usually mean that she is a very kind person. Why discuss it then if everyone knows what it is and if everyone values it. Most people think that they practice it or at least try to for most of the time. Kindness is such an ordinary thing but it does make a big impact on peoples lives. We frequently do not realise how important it is.

One of the first women that I visited when I started work in a church in a town in northern England, who has since died, lived alone, had no close relatives was afflicted by illness and constant pain. She could not escape from the four walls of her small apartment but she was appreciative of being surrounded by a mass of kindness. Kindness flowed into her life from neighbours and friends. They were all people who she had helped years ago and who were eager, and enthusiastic to repay to overflowing the kindness that had been shown to them. She very rarely asked for anything for herself but they would always help her out. And even though she sometimes got depressed and upset because she could no longer get out and was so dependent on others, she was carried along by a wave of kindness. Without this she would not have been able to continue in her own home. Kindness enabled her to cope. The old saying was proved true again; you don't know who your friends are until you are in need or trouble.

Kindness is:

Kindness is not only a fruit of the spirit in the lives of Christians, but also is a beautiful word expressing a beautiful idea. It is love in action. (as Paul said in 1 Cor 13.4 "*Love is patient, love is kind*") Kindness is about being as concerned about another person's well-being as we are about our own.

I am sure that we all can think of examples we have known. The couple who were victims of an arson attack on their home. They lost everything but church friends and secular neighbours rallied round and not only fitted them out with everything that they had lost but even found them a house which was empty to stay in. The man who's wife's sudden death left him in such a state of shock that he could hardly do anything for himself. He found his friends and neighbours came round to do everything for him for those first few days when he couldn't face doing anything. And he said to me "I didn't know people were so kind."

It is about looking outwards rather than inwards. It is about not putting your own needs first. To do so can often result in selfishness and this is being unkind. As it says in the book of Proverbs 12:25 "*Worries depress a man but a kind word cheers him up.*"

God is kind...

Like so many virtues we are attempting to be like God and put on his virtues and grow in his likeness. We sing the old hymn "Let us with a gladsome mind, praise the Lord for he is kind" The Jewish bible gives a clear message that God is kind. *"I am the Lord who exercises kindness"* (Jer 9:24) *"You are kind and forgiving O Lord"* (Ps 86:5) *"God shows unfailing kindness to his anointed."* (Ps 18:50)

Indeed when Jesus is teaching about loving your enemies he makes the point that we should do this because of the way that God loves. Thus Jesus says in Luke 6.35 we should love our enemies because God *"is kind to the ungrateful and wicked"* Saying God is kind doesn't mean that God is always nice to us, or always gives us what we want. It does mean that he loves us and wants the best for us. It means that he loves all people equally and wants all people to turn to him and it means that God's love is real and focused in real action.

We've all heard the saying you've got to be cruel to be kind. It is usually said by a parent who knows that giving in to her child's every whim won't do them any good. We often think this is the way God works too. God tempers his mercy with Justice. God isn't just a vending machine in the sky where we put in a prayer and out will come your hearts desire. We can't manipulate God. God loves us and if his idea of kindness doesn't fall in with our wishes then it is our idea of God that is wrong and not God's love.

We see that Jesus taught kindness in the story of the good Samaritan. Here Jesus revealed that kindness to our neighbours is what we should all aim for and that everyone is our neighbour. Such kindness goes beyond doing what is expected and especially regarding those who are to be in receipt of our kindness.

Kindness is something for all but especially for Christians to show. The word keeps cropping up in the New Testament. Listen to teachings to the early church. *"Be kind and compassionate"* (Eph 4:32) *"but always try and be kind to each other"* (1Th 5:15) *"instead he must be kind to everyone."* (2Tim 2:24) They obviously needed telling. They can't have been very good at it. But then I expect the church in Ephesus or Thessilonica was just like the church here that we know well. The church made up of an odd bunch of people, some of whom you get on with and others who you just can't seem to understand. There will be people who behave differently and others who believe differently. God's message is simply be kind to one another. Tolerant. The truth of God that unites us is much bigger than the things that divide us.

Kindness is often done in secret. When Brian Clough the football manager announced his retirement I heard to a radio commentator summing up his often loud and outspoken career. He said Clough was a man who has done many kind things to numerous of people in private and not made any fuss. Kindness shouldn't attract publicity. If it does then it is being done for the wrong reasons.

Kindness is reciprocal

We receive as we give, and we receive far more than we give. As we give to others so God gives to us. Again the book of proverbs illustrates this well. *"A Kind man benefits himself"*

(Prov11:17) *"blessed is he who is kind to the needy"* (Prov14:21) *"whoever is kind to the needy honours God"* (Prov 14:31)

Being kind to others, especially those in need, brings blessings on us ourselves and honours God. It also benefits ourselves as we grow in Godlikeness.

Kindness is one of the first ways that Christians are judged by those outside the church. Kindness like unkindness is one of the things that can either make or mar your first impression of a person. It can't be pretended. It is love in action. It is something that is desperately needed in our world, society, and local community today. Kindness is about showing true friendship and what it means to love your neighbour as yourself.

Kindness is a way we can show that to be a Christian does make a difference in the world. When we are being good neighbours in a world where people don't expect anything from their neighbours. Showing we care when people don't expect you to bother. This sort of behaviour gets Christians noticed as different. The fruit of the spirit working in our lives should make a difference and this is a real practical difference that can be seen.

As a fruit of the spirit, kindness should be one of the lovely graces that is evident in the life of a growing, alive and developing Christian.

6 GOODNESS

Introduction

One of the things said most frequently to children is "be good". But at the same time I remember that at school the one person that no one really liked was the "goody goody" person who was often also considered the teachers pet.

Goodness is commended to us as a fruit of the spirit. As such goodness is something more than a description of correct moral behaviour. Goodness is a broad, morally positive concept but it typically deals with life, charity, continuity, happiness, love, prosperity and justice. Goodness is difficult to define but easy to recognise in character or conduct

Goodness is a quality that is more than just doing what is right. Goodness can be seen in the lives of some of the saints. (One contemporary figure that comes immediately to mind is Mother Theresa) It is a special quality that makes their life stand out as different. It is something that is deep in the core of the personality. It is really about being like God.

God's goodness

The bible is full of references to the goodness of God. Here are a few examples.

"Good and upright is the Lord, therefore he instructs sinners in his ways" (Ps 25:8)

"The Lord is good, a refuge in times of trouble. He cares for those who trust in him" (Na 1:7)

"Taste and see that the lord is good; blessed is the man who takes refuge in him" (Ps 34: 8)

"Why do you ask me about what is good? Jesus replied, There is only one who is good. If you want to enter life obey the commandments" (Mt 19:17)

There are also many references to doing good, such as:

"Trust in the lord and do good. Dwell in the land and enjoy safe pasture" (Ps 37:7)

"And do not forget to do good and to share with others, for with such sacrifices God is pleased." (Heb 13:16)

"Anyone who knows the good he ought to do and doesn't do it sins." (James 4.17)

"But love your enemies do goo to them and lend to them without expecting to get anything back. Then your reward will be great, and you will be sons of the most high because he is kind to the ungrateful and wicked." (Luke 6.35)

The vision of God's goodness will frequently impel us to work for change or to see right and wrong more clearly. It will save us from being too narrow in our thinking or our loving and will enable us to see others with greater understanding and compassion.

Goodness is holiness

In Trollop's epic novel “Barchester Towers” Septimus Harding is the character who appears the most mature and the most good. Yet he himself is always conscious of his own failings and what he sees as his lack of charity. Such humility is one of the marks of a truly good person. Unlike the false humility that is epitomised by Charles Dicken's character Uriah Heap. If we so order our lives to keep a vision always before us of God, then other events, and people and priorities will fall into proper perspective. As a result we shall be less and less preoccupied with own concerns and more and more occupied with other peoples needs and their claims on us.

Do you remember the old hymn that is very rarely heard these days? "Teach us how to grow in goodness". Regrettably there is no short cut to growing in goodness. We have to be prepared to change and mature through a lifetime if we are to attain all the goodness which we long for. The goodness that loves people not because of their attractiveness or abilities or achievement but because they are themselves unique beings loved by God.

This is hard. Some people are naturally unlovely and seemingly unlovable. I asked a guy I know who works with homeless people how he manages to love them all, even the most smelly and unpleasant. He said I talk to them. I ask them about themselves and talk about their lives. And for every one I have bothered to spend time with, I have found something in their wild chaotic lives that is likeable. I remember that one thing. And I use that one thing as a way in to think of them as a fellow human being. Once I have done that I can not help but love them, no matter how much they smell.

Goodness in our own lives manifests itself as we are genuine warm and accepting of others. As we centre ourselves more and more on the goodness of God, we are all the more able to see the needs of and help our neighbours. Goodness is a transforming reality in the lives of all who are faced with the many and varied things that are not good. Goodness is not an unattainable goal.

In our journey towards goodness even though our thoughts and wills are directed heavenwards our feet must be kept firmly on the ground of our daily experience. This will allow the fruit of goodness to mature for the benefit of ourselves and of others. In the lines of another old hymn:

Holy spirit dwell with me
I myself would holy be
Separate from sin I would
choose and cherish all things good.

7 FAITHFULNESS

The faithfulness of God is emphasised many times in the bible and in this popular hymn.

"Great is Thy faithfulness, O God my Father...
Morning by morning new mercies I see.
All I have needed Thy hand hath provided.
Great is Thy faithfulness, Lord, unto me."

There are more than sixty references in the bible to the faithfulness of God and it's not surprising that some forty of these instances occur in the book of Psalms. Here are recorded the struggles of the people of God and their total dependence upon God at times for His faithfulness. They show that they were dependent upon God's faithfulness for everything. For example, *"I will sing of the mercies of the Lord forever; with my mouth will I make known Your faithfulness to all generations. For I have said, Mercy shall be built up forever; Your faithfulness You shall establish in the very heavens."* (Psalm 89:1-2)

What is faithfulness?

The biblical word denotes that which is firm and can be counted upon. Webster's dictionary defines faithful as "firm in adherence to promises or an observance of duty." Some common synonyms are: dependable, reliable, trustworthy and loyal. The word also implies "absolute honesty and integrity."

From these pictures of God we get a picture of what the fruit of faithfulness means for us. A faithful person is not only honest and dependable, but also loyal.

Jesus similarly promises faithfulness to his followers in the gospels. Every time you gather to worship with brothers & sisters as Christians, we remember that He said, *"Where two or three come together in my name, there am I with them"* (Matthew 18:20). Every time we take holy communion, we remember that He said, *"I will be with you always, even to the end of the world."* And when we are faced with death we remember His promise, *"In my Father's house are many rooms...I am going there to prepare a place for you. And if I go and prepare a place for you, I will come back and take you to be with me. For where I am, there you will be also"* (Matthew 14:2-4)

Faithfulness is to follow through with a commitment regardless of difficulty. Faithfulness has been defined as love hanging on. It is love saying, I will not quit. There may be misunderstandings, there may be disappointments, and there may be discouragements, but I will not quit. Ever.

In the New Testament our faithfulness is frequently challenged.

We are challenged to be faithful in stewardship in 1 Corinthians 4:1-2.

We are challenged to be faithful in service in Ephesians 6:21.

We are challenged to be faithful in our marriages in 1 Timothy 5:9.

We are challenged to be faithful in witnessing in Revelation 2:15.

We are challenged to be faithful in prayer in Romans 12:12.

We are challenged to be faithful in ministry in Colossians 1:7.

We are challenged to be faithful in following the Lord in Revelation 17:14.

We are challenged to be faithful in the truth in 3John 3.

We are challenged to be faithful even in times of persecution in Revelation 13:10.

We are challenged to be faithful unto death and then we'll receive the crown of life in Revelation 2:10.

There will be many examples that all of us can draw from everyday life where we are called upon to be faithful - honest, dependable, loyal and filled with integrity. We could list some here: marriage, business relationships, friendship, family life, in making promises, in legal contracts and in fact we can see it applies to virtually every part of life that you can think of.

In the gospels Simon Peter often made mistakes. He was impetuous. He even denied Jesus and then wept bitterly out of shame for what he had done. But when he fell down he was able to get up, dust himself off and start all over again. And because of this faithfulness he was chosen by Jesus for a special role and became one of the leaders of the disciples after Jesus' death. God was at work through Peter and God will work through us if we can show the same faithfulness through adversity and failure.

Faithfulness to God includes faithfulness to one another. When we look at the two great commandments we see that we are to love God first, but then love our neighbour as our self. The two commandments go together and should always be seen together. God requires that we be faithful to Him and also to each other in our daily lives. God shows faithfulness and God also expects and blesses our faithfulness.

8 GENTLENESS

As a child I used to sing the hymn "Gentle Jesus meek and mild" which today has been expurgated from the hymn book. As a lad I imagined the Jesus described by the opening line in those adjectives to be an insipid, weak and soft character. Yet the word gentle occurs in the scriptures several times, describing Jesus and the activities of the apostles. *"As apostles of Christ we could have been a burden to you, but we were gentle among you, like a mother caring for her little children."* (1Th2:7) Gentleness is obviously something more than the soft long and strong roll of toilet tissue that a cute puppy cavorts among on a television advertisement.

What Gentleness is not:

The word gentleman now seems old fashioned. It is not even used on public conveniences any more; we are now men or a symbol in trousers. But we all still know what is meant if someone is described as a real gentleman, or a proper gent. They are describing a man, and usually an older man who is well mannered, lifts his hat when he meets people, stands when a lady enters the room, automatically treats every woman as a duchess, and generally seems rather a quaint reminder of the days gone by when we like to believe that this land was a nicer, friendlier place, and where people showed respect. But gentleness as a fruit of the spirit is not about manners and codes of conduct.

A very similar word to gentle is the word genteel. A word that originally meant well bred: graceful in manners and form but as my dictionary reminded me it is now "used with mocking reference to a standard of obsolete snobbery or false refinement." Unfortunately the term genteel in this mocking tone is often used to caricature the church by people who have no contact with it. They portray it as an institution that promotes cucumber sandwich eating garden parties filled with characters straight out of Agatha Christie's Miss Marple novels, set in a fictitious rural idyll that never existed. Gentleness in such a portrayal is seen to be the prerogative of the nearly extinct breed of gentlefolk, usually including an upper-class unworldly parish vicar. This is not what the bible is suggesting either.

In several places the bible commends gentleness as the way that Christians should behave towards one another. What this actually means in practice I will examine later but first it seems to me that the reason that we are commanded to be gentle with one another is that we are being called to mirror the way God behaves towards us.

God is gentle with us:

When the prophet Isaiah wrote God *"will feed his flock like a shepherd, he will gather the lambs into his arms, he will carry them in his bosom, and gently lead those that are with young"* (Isa 40:11) he was describing the behaviour of God towards his people in terms of a gentle loving affection. Sometimes we are led to believe that the Old Testament picture of God concentrates solely on his strength and warlike characteristics. Indeed the verse the one I have just quoted before emphasised this very point: *"behold, the lord your God comes with might, and his arm rules for Him"* (Isa 40:10) In verse 11 though God is almost described as a pet lover to put it in modern terms. The sheep though were not pets. They had a purpose, a function, they were part of a commercial enterprise and the whole shepherds livelihood depended on them. The shepherd had to take care of them to get the best out of them. Modern farmers are coming to realise that contented animals produce better yields. I heard a while ago of a company that sells special footballs for pigs. Pigs in modern indoor pig farms get very bored because they don't go outside and often only have a limited space in which to live. As a result they often have fights and hurt each other. But if they are given a football they play with it and use up their surplus energy in that way. Animals that work for us have to be cared for. The prophet Isaiah told of the gentleness of the shepherd. God wants to get the best out of us and so he gently cares for us too.

Isaiah also refers to God's gentleness when he says *"a bruised reed he will not break and a dimly burning wick he will not quench."* (Isa 42:3) Here God's gentleness is pictured using descriptions of two of the most fragile things known to the writer. A bruised reed which is so fine, and easy to be broken, yet God does not break it, and a smoldering candle which the lightest breath would extinguish, yet God does not snuff it out. When I was a child I used to watch the manic game programme "Its a Knock out" on the television. Different teams would compete in crazy games, usually involving getting wet and covered with foam. One of the games sticks in my mind: drivers of mechanical JCV diggers had to pick up eggs and put them in boxes using the great big mechanical digger back fill shovel that they usually use for lifting great shovelfuls of earth out of trenches that they have been digging. Imagine these huge, powerful machines, picking up what are the most fragile of objects an egg. The skilled operators managed to move quite a number of eggs from a tray into an egg box without breaking them. Here was a machine of great power and strength but used with great gentleness. Or perhaps you have seen the James Bond film "Moonraker". The film has one particularly memorable character, a big seven foot tall henchman thug, known as Jaws on account of his metal teeth. In the movie he falls in love with a young woman who has the distinguishing feature of heavy braces on her teeth to match his metal jaws. There is a scene where the big villain turns into a romantic hero as violins play in the background and their eyes meet and they gently cross over the rubble from some spectacular stunt that has just crashed all around them and fall into each others arms. A moment of memorable high comedy. Yet God is said to be like this. Powerful beyond all our imaginings yet as gentle with us as is possible.

Indeed it was in gentle ways that God often chose to communicate. Think of the time when the prophet Elijah had run away and hid in a cave (1Kings19). There came strong wind, earthquake, and then fire and God was not in any of them but *"after the fire came a gentle whisper"* (1 Kings 19:12 NIV) and Gods voice was in the gentle whisper.

St Paul, when he wrote to the church in Corinth thought that the gentleness of Jesus was one his most important attributes. He uses these characteristics to command their attention when he wrote *"I Paul, myself entreat you, by the meekness and gentleness of Christ...."* (2Cor10:1). He thought that Jesus' gentleness was so important that it was something that he should use in his argument and draw special attention to it.

So God is gentle with us, his people, but gentleness is not softness. he commands us to be gentle with one another in the same way.

We should be gentle with one another:

The wisdom of the Book of Proverbs commends gentleness as a pragmatic way of behaving. That book of the Bible is full of what today would be recognised as sound common sense. *"A gentle answer turns away wrath, but a harsh word stirs up anger."*(Prov 15:1) We know that to be the case when dealing with others. If you are returning faulty goods to a shop we all know from experience that we get a better response if we are calm and persistent than those times when we lose our temper or shout and gesticulate wildly.

"As apostles of Christ we could have been a burden to you, but we were gentle among you, like a mother caring for her little children." (1Th2:7) In Thessalonians Paul describes the gentleness that he and the other apostles had when they worked in the church among them. The gentleness described here is the gentleness of a nurse for a baby or small child. When you first become a parent you are very aware that babies are delicate and have to be handled with care. When I was a new father I was very nervous about handling my new born child. She looked so small and delicate. But a nurses experienced hands know just how firmly to hold a small child - too gently and they wriggle out of your grasp, but on the other hand if you hold them too firmly you could bruise them. The nurse

reassured me and told me to grip firmly because we the baby had experienced considerable forces and pressures during the process of being born and normal handling was much gentler than this!

In this way we can begin to see that gentleness with one another is not softness: *"And the Lord's servant must not be quarrelsome but kindly to everyone, an apt teacher, forbearing, correcting his opponents with gentleness"* (2Tim 2:24-25). In this part of St Paul's letter to Timothy gentleness is linked to to a certain amount of firmness, which, couched in educational terms, is seen to be for the child's own good. Being gentle doesn't imply giving in all the time, being used by others. A Christian is called to be a servant but that does not mean being a doormat. We are not there for people to wipe their feet on! Gentleness doesn't mean giving in when you are in the right, but being firm and sticking to your guns. Gentleness is part of the total approach of a Christian. It is about a Christians attitude to the whole of life. You can be gentle and assertive at the same time.

James letter makes gentleness part of the good works that show themselves in the lives of a christian *"Who is wise and understanding among you? let him show his works in the meekness of wisdom...... the wisdom from above is first pure then peaceable, gentle, open to reason, full of mercy and good fruits, without uncertainty or insincerity."*(James3:13&17). Gentleness implies consideration, fairness, and understanding in your approach to others. This may sound a bit like an iron fist in a kid glove but it is not because the motivation is always love. You correct a child from doing something that would bring them harm because of your love for them. So too we have to be strict as Christians for that which is right, and although we are gentle with the sinner we hate the sin, to quote an old saying.

As a fruit of the spirit, gentleness shows in us as the Holy spirit works inside us. So gentleness with one another is something we should expect to find in the church, and we would want to encourage. Being gentle doesn't mean being a pushover or a soft touch but it does mean dealing with all people and all things in love as God deals with us

9 SELF CONTROL

Of all the fruits of the spirit, the one that seems to have the least to be said about it seems to be self control. Everyone knows what self control is. It is being in control of yourself. It is not getting carried away by passionate outbursts and being in command of your emotions and your actions. The bible promises that this is something that is a fruit of life in Christ. A fruit of the Holy Spirit. But what really is it?

I started thinking about this and wondered if a Christian is really a cool character who never shows any emotions, never gets heated, never is ruffled at whatever life throws up and never gets angry. If we were to look at self control in this way then rather than a grace, it would be more of a straightjacket into which we would have to button ourselves.

Self control is something that is essential for everyone. When I was writing this the house was tidy ready for the arrival of a young couple for a pre-wedding interview. Then my 2 year old daughter tipped all her bricks over the floor where the meeting was to be held. After I had cleared them up I saw that she had crayoned on the glass of the patio doors. There was no point in getting really angry with her as there is a limit to what she can understand. You can't reason with a child of that age to tell them why they shouldn't behave in that way. So, difficult as it sometimes is, you have to have self control. The bible says *"A man without self control is like a city broken into and left without walls"*(Prov 25:28) In the ancient days of fortified cities, the whole safety and prosperity of a town depended on its walls. If the walls were breached the town was open to marauding bandits and pillaging thieves. It was no longer a place of safety. It was no longer good for the purpose for which it was built. Likewise the book of Proverbs tells us that with out self control a person`is no longer good for the purpose for which they have been created.

One thing that is traditionally said to be very English is to have a stiff upper lip. I am rather puzzled by this phrase though as it seems to me that the upper lip isn't the place where most of our emotions show. Having a stiff upper lip is about keeping all your feelings hidden, keeping calm and unflustered on the outside irrespective of whatever you may be feeling on the inside. It was certainly the way to behave in the Victorian age. It was a characteristic that the British Empire was said to be founded on. In many other places today where Victorian values continue, it is still thought to be wrong for men to show their feelings in public and also rather unseemly for women to make an exhibition of their passions. Now this is not the same as the self control that is commended as a cardinal virtue in the bible.

Nowhere in the bible does Jesus tell people that they should pretend to be or not to be, or pretend to feel or not feel something false. Jesus' message of salvation was about wholeness, and this implies an integrity in the total person. Having a stiff upper lip is about deceiving people and acting falsely. A stiff upper lip isn't a description of self control – it is a description of being a good actor who keeps calm and on message in spite of the distractions of life.

If we use the word self discipline then we are getting closer to the meaning. I read recently about a lifer. A lifer is a prisoner sentenced to life imprisonment for murder. She kept herself going inside prison by reading long classical novels and Shakespeare's plays. She rationed herself to two Shakespeare plays a year and would only read two chapters of a book by a favourite author each day to make these works lasted longer. In this way she made sure that she had enough reading matter to last out her sentence. She had to have something to look forward to and this self imposed rationing of her reading allowed her to look forward to some good reading in the years ahead that she knew would be behind bars.

But that sort of strong will power isn't the sort of self control either that was talked about as a cardinal virtue or fruit of the spirit, though it can be found in the bible. In the story of Daniel, for example, the young men who were being educated by King Nebuchadnezzar exercised strong self discipline. *"Daniel resolved that he would not defile himself with the kings rich food and wine"* (Daniel 1:8) They behaved in this way to show the king that their strength came from God and not from the rich diet that they were being fed. They didn't do it to show that they could do it through the strength of their willpower.

The Greek word that is translated as self control can also be translated as temperance. A proper understanding of that word, which now sounds old fashioned, is very helpful to us. Temperance is usually associated with not drinking alcohol but in the Bible the self control or temperance called for is for much more than this. The scope of the need for temperance can be seen in the lists of things that should be avoided because they are harmful to the character and the spirit. The letters to the early churches are full of warnings concerning the characteristics of the opposite of temperance such as lust (1 Cor 7:5) drunkenness (1 Tim 3:3) quarreling, lying, boastfulness, greed (1 Tim 3:8) and conceit (1 Tim 3:6). All parts of the body are to be controlled and there is even a whole chapter in the letter of James devoted to the control of the tongue. (James 3)

If we use the word temperance instead of self control and say that a person should be temperate in all things, what then does this mean? Temperance is about living in a way where you control what can be controlled and not attempting to control that which cannot be controlled. It is about the whole of life and it shows itself in a persons attitude to their life.

Intemperance could be said to be found in someone who is a scatter brain: someone who thinks too much too quickly, and about too many subjects. On the other hand temperance implies a state of mind where you can think quietly and coolly and thus much more profoundly. A temperate person has the peace of mind to think problems and issues through properly.

An intemperate person will talk too much and to too many people. They may take too many people into their intimate confidences. The warning in the letter of James about the tongue is particularly relevant here. But if you are temperate you will listen carefully to what other people say to you and only talk about subjects that are relevant. In this way you discuss your family finances with your family alone, but you discuss the state of your lawn with anyone who stops and chats with you at the front of the house! Do you remember the occasion when, towards the end of his life, Jesus was called before the High Priest and questioned. Jesus remained silent. (Matt 26:63) He knew there was no point in answering back so he remained silent. As it says in the book of Ecclesiastes there is *"a time to keep silence and a time to speak"* (Eccles 3:7)

An intemperate person is too grateful, too sympathetic and perhaps also too prone to give advice. A temperate person does these things in proportion to the circumstances. No one takes seriously someone who always goes over the top with their praise or condolences! They just say "Yes yes its only him going on again". No one really listens to the advice of someone who is always telling everyone else what to do.

Intemperance is about getting involved in too many things, because you cannot say no, and as a result nothing is done well. On the other hand a temperate person will be quite ruthless in selecting out what things should be done and can be done well and then concentrating on doing them. If we see temperance or self control in this way rather than a burden it shows itself to be common sense.

Self control or temperance isn't easy to achieve. It frightens some people. They are discouraged from attempting temperance because it sounds difficult but this has always been the case as St Paul found when preaching before Felix. *"And as he argued about justice and self control and future judgement Felix was alarmed and said 'Go away for the present.'"* (Acts 24:25) We are put off trying to achieve self control even though we can see that it is a good thing, and even though it is something that we admire in others.

Nevertheless, however difficult it may seem to be, however daunting, it is something that we are clearly instructed to do. Peter's first letter tells us *"Therefore gird up your minds, be sober, set your hope fully upon the grace that is coming to you at the revelation of Jesus Christ."* (1 Peter 1:13). Peter indeed went further that this. In common with other Christians at that time he expected the immediate end of the world when he wrote *"The end of all things is near. You must be self controlled and alert to be able to pray."* (1 Peter 4:7) But he clearly linked the ability to be able to pray with being self controlled. This is because when we come to God in prayer our wholeness or lack of it is shown up in the light of God's presence. Our wholeness, the integration of our personalities, comes from showing temperance in all things, including in the practice of temperance. There is nothing worse than someone who takes temperance to extremes and is so hard on themselves that the more they think they are suffering the more good they think it is doing.

I mentioned earlier that the word temperance used to be associated exclusively with alcohol and the temperance movement. In a way though all things that are done to excess can become addictive narcotics to an intemperate person. Over work, over talking, in the same way as over drinking can all be drugs to dull the edges of fear and stop someone from thinking about what is happening to them, within them and through them. People can take drugs, talk too much, overwork, and drink excessively when they cannot face up to themselves. In this way many forms of intemperate behaviour can be said to be symptoms of an underlying spiritual, emotional or psychological problem.

But this is something that we do not have to struggle with in our own strength. For God wants us to behave with temperance in all things and God will help us to achieve this. The writer to the Ephesians puts it clearly when he writes *"I ask God from the wealth of his glory, to give you power through his spirit to be strong in your inner-selves"* (Eph 3:16) God will help us to achieve that which is impossible for us to achieve on our own. In this way we to come to know the love of Christ which surpasses knowledge and we can be filled with all the fullness of God to complete the promise in this chapter of Ephesians.

10 WELL-BEING AS WHOLENESS AND THE FRUITS OF THE SPIRIT

This book has looked at each of the fruits of the spirit in turn and now it is time to consider what they result in when put together in one life. As I wrote these chapters I was aware of the way they are all related and fit together to build up a picture of what life should be like.

Wholeness is difficult to define. It is related to holiness but is different and can be used with integrity in a completely secular setting.

Its an important issue for many people as they eat their wholefoods and try to take a wholistic or holistic view of health care, and look for an integration of body mind and spirit. As I said in the introduction the Hebrew word shalom is helpful for our understanding as its meaning includes all of the following: completeness, wholeness, health, peace, welfare, soundness, tranquility, prosperity, perfectness, fullness, rest, and harmony. In other words it is the absence of disharmony, agitation, dis-ease and disease, and fragmentation. Shalom involves awareness of our oneness with our God, as known to us in the trinity of Father, Son and Holy Spirit, and with one another. That is a helpful place to start because we can see these characteristics as being positive aspects of life associated with wholeness and well-being.

The insight of the list of fruits of the spirit from the book of Galatians is also very helpful in this debate. The nine fruits love, joy, peace, patience, kindness, goodness, faithfulness, gentleness, and self-control suggest a way of living which is at harmony with those around you. It is a way of life that is not aggressive or controlling yet in command and assertive. This is the deep meaning of the phrase used by Jesus "I have come to bring life and life in all fullness" - this is fullness of life.

If these characteristics are all present in a person who I would recognise them as someone who had "got it all together" and was fully human. When I use the phrase fully human I mean that this is someone you look at and say "life should be lived like that". The supreme example that each of us tries to follow is Jesus Christ. In his life and especially in his interactions with other people Jesus as recorded in the gospels shows us many examples of how to react and behave and live as whole, fully human beings.

The challenge that Jesus gives to us is to act with self emptying generosity. This is not an intellectual or even a moral challenge. It is a challenge of the imagination. It is a challenge that calls on us to think of "what might be if...." As a result of thinking like this we create new possibilities that are counter cultural, counter intuitive and certainly not what society expects.

And it is inevitable that we are hesitant to follow the example of Jesus as counter intuitive and counter cultural action needs courage. By pausing before we act we are given time to override our gut reactions, hard wired into our brain as survival mechanisms, alongside fight or flight, appetite and motor movement.

When struggling to follow Jesus we pause and say a little prayer and in that moment we can move from the primitive gut reactions in the core of our hard wired brain to the graced wisdom that allows us to choose to do something that is not dictated by narrow survival thinking.

In the life and teaching of Jesus we can see many examples of counter intuitive and counter cultural action, graced by God. We need to study the life and teaching of Jesus to open our imaginations to the possibilities of living and acting in a completely different way. The gospels are a wonderful resource for the graced, generous imagination and studying the life of Jesus will help us to develop new ways of living.

In the secular world the concept of well-being is a live issue. For example, "The Guardian" newspaper on Friday fifteenth July 2011 had an article on happiness at work. People are not just motivated by money. The top motivator is "respect" – how much employees feel valued and trusted by their organisation. Then comes (in order of priority) "type of work", "providing good service to customers", "the people you work with" and finally, good "work-life balance". It suggested five ways to make workplaces happier environments. First, we need managers with better social and interpersonal skills, who manage people by praise and reward and not fault-finding (because few managers do this, a pay rise is often the only time people feel their contribution is recognised). Second, individuals should have autonomy and control over their work – the absence of micro-management. Third, there needs to be a shorter working hours culture, where appropriate flexible working arrangements are available which people can take up without damaging their careers or feeling guilty. Fourth, there should be manageable workloads and achievable deadlines, and finally, a culture should be encouraged in which employees feel valued and trusted. Well-being is related to wholeness in that I see the fruits of the spirit present in a good healthy workplace as described in this newspaper article.

Well-being can be split down into: emotional, spiritual, social and financial well-being.

Emotional well-being encompasses mood, self-efficacy, self-image, and such like. It is essentially about your feelings, viewpoint and confidence in yourself.

Spiritual well-being centers on your relationship with God and the activities that support and enhance this relationship such as prayer, meditation, bible study and worship.

Social well-being considers the relationships within your life including support from friends and family. Do we live in a healthy and supportive community?

Financial well-being considers how well one is managing the business of living as well as preparing for retirement. While financial well-being is not often an element included in models of health, it is often a source of stress which can have major effects on multiple dimensions of health.

Each one of these components, when in their optimal state, helps to ensure the overall well-being and effectiveness of the human being. When one or more are impaired, the overall health and vitality of the individual suffers and their ability to thrive is diminished.

Each of the fruits of the spirit can be seen as contributing to one or more of the four types of well-being identified above. To spell out the obvious:

For our emotional well-being we need love, joy, peace, patience, kindness, goodness, faithfulness, gentleness, and self-control.

For our spiritual well-being we need love, joy, peace, patience, kindness, goodness, faithfulness, gentleness, and self-control.

In our social well-being we need love, joy, peace, patience, kindness, goodness, faithfulness, gentleness, and self-control.

And even to achieve financial well-being we need love, joy, peace, patience, kindness, goodness, faithfulness, gentleness, and self-control.

The fruits of the spirit are indispensable to wholeness, well-being and experiencing fulness of life.

I will conclude this small book with a prayer that I need to pray regularly.

A prayer

Heavenly father, You have shown us how life is to be lived through your word and in the example of Jesus. Help us to study and meditate on all your messages to us that we might learn to live in the way of Christ and show the fruits of the spirit in our lives. Send your Holy Spirit to help us because on our own we all find it difficult to do what you would have us do.

We pray in the name of Jesus. Amen.

ABOUT THE AUTHOR

Pastor John started working as a church minister in 1988 in the north of England. Since then he has worked in rural, suburban and city centre churches with large and small congregations. He thinks the work of a pastor is the best job in the world and has gained some wisdom in his years of ministry. He tries to live in the fruit of the spirit but like all disciples he often fails to live up to the example of Jesus. John is now lives in central Scotland with his wife, mother and two dogs. He enjoys walking, gardening and photography in his spare time. He and his wife of 28 years have two grown up children who were toddlers when he started writing this book!

10553243R00039

Printed in Great Britain
by Amazon.co.uk, Ltd.,
Marston Gate.